GOD GOD GOD
SAVE SAVE SAVE
THE
QUEEN QU

C000057014

GOD
SAVE SAVE SAVE
THE THE THE
QUEEN QUEEN QUEEN

GOD GOD GOD
SAVE SAVE SAVE
THE THE THE
QUEEN QUEEN QU

GOD GOD GOD
SAVE SAVE SAVE
THE THE THE
QUEEN QUEEN QUEEN

GOD
SAVE
THE
QUEEN

GOD
SAVE
THE
QUEEN

GOD
SAVE
THE
QUEEN

GOD
SAVE
THE
QUEEN

GOD
SAVE
THE
QUEEN

GOD
SAVE
THE
QUEEN

GOD
SAVE
THE
QUEEN

GOD
SAVE
THE
QUEEN

GOD
SAVE
THE
QUEEN

GOD
SAVE
THE
QUEEN

GOD SAVE THE QUEEN

Summersdale Publishers Ltd
46 West Street
Chichester
West Sussex
PO19 1RP
UK

www.summersdale.com

Printed and bound in Czech Republic

ISBN: 978-1-84953-3010

Substantial discounts on bulk quantities of Summersdale books are available to corporations, professional associations and other organisations. For details telephone Summersdale Publishers on (+44-1243-771107), fax (+44-1243-786300) or email (nicky@summersdale.com).

Disclaimer
Every effort has been made to provide accurate information in this collection. Should there be any omissions or errors in this respect we apologise and shall be pleased to rectify these in any future edition.

GOD
SAVE
THE
QUEEN

summersdale

CONTENTS

ESSENTIAL FACTS ABOUT QUEEN ELIZABETH II

In the United Kingdom, Her Majesty's official title is Her Majesty Elizabeth the Second, by the Grace of God, of the United Kingdom of Great Britain and Northern Ireland, and of Her other Realms and Territories, Queen, Head of the Commonwealth, Defender of the Faith.

Princess Elizabeth Alexandra Mary,
later to become Queen Elizabeth II,
was born at 2.40 a.m. on 21 April 1926
at 17 Bruton Street, Mayfair, London.

The Queen's star sign is Taurus.

Elizabeth was named after her mother, the former Lady Elizabeth Bowes-Lyon, while her two middle names are those of her paternal great-grandmother Queen Alexandra and grandmother Queen Mary, respectively.

Her full title at birth was Her Royal Highness Princess Elizabeth of York.

At birth, the Queen was third in line to the throne behind her uncle, who later became King Edward VIII, and her father, later King George VI. She was not expected to become queen.

When her uncle Edward VIII abdicated because of his intended marriage to Wallis Simpson, Elizabeth's father became king, and she became heiress presumptive at the age of ten.

If her parents had had a son, he would have been next in line to the throne.

Queen Elizabeth II's father, King
George VI, died on 6 February 1952.
She was staying at Treetops Hotel
in Kenya at the time, and returned to
England immediately upon hearing
the news. She signed her Accession
document two days later on 8 February.

The person who told the Queen
of the death of her father and
her accession to the throne was
her husband, Prince Philip.

Queen Elizabeth II is the second-longest-reigning monarch, after Queen Victoria – her great-great-grandmother.

Queen Elizabeth II is the second-longest-reigning current monarch and head of state, after King Bhumibol Adulyadej of Thailand.

She is the twelfth monarch of Great
Britain since the 1707 Act of Union
between England and Scotland…

… and the fortieth monarch
since William the Conqueror
took the throne in 1066.

Like Queen Victoria, the Queen has been on the throne for such a long time that she has required a second Great Seal to be made, after the first one wore out. The Great Seal is used for approving state documents.

CHILDHOOD AND YOUTH

As a child, the Princess Elizabeth
was affectionately known as
'Lilibet' by her family.

Elizabeth and her sister were educated at home by their governess Marion Crawford, known as 'Crawfie'.

In the early years of her life, Elizabeth lived quietly with her family at the Royal Lodge in Windsor Great Park, until 1937 when her father was crowned.

The young Princess Elizabeth had her
own small house on the grounds of the
Royal Lodge, given to her by the people
of Wales in 1932, called Y Bwthyn
Bach (Welsh for 'The Little Cottage').

As a child, she enjoyed acting
in pantomimes performed
at Windsor Castle.

Princess Elizabeth was also a keen swimmer in her childhood. She won the Children's Challenge Shield at London's Bath Club at the age of thirteen.

In May 1939 Princesses Elizabeth and Margaret travelled for the first time on the London Underground, accompanied by their governess.

The Girl Guides 1st Buckingham
Palace Company was formed when
Princess Elizabeth became a Girl
Guide. It was made up of Palace
employees' children and young
members of the Royal Household.

During the London Blitz in 1940,
Princess Elizabeth and her sister
Princess Margaret were moved to
Windsor Castle for their safety.

PHOTOGRAPHS AND PORTRAITS

Four different portraits of the Queen
have been used on UK coinage
since the first coin depicting Her
Majesty was issued in 1953. The
most recent portrait was in 1998 by
the sculptor Ian Rank-Broadley.

It is believed that the image of Her Majesty by Arnold Machin, used on British coins between 1968 and 1984, and on British postage stamps from 1967 to the present day, is the most reproduced work of art in history.

Since 1960, all Bank of England banknotes issued have featured a portrait of the Queen facing left, and a watermark image which shows her facing right.

In her lifetime, the Queen has sat for over 129 official portraits. Her very first portrait was commissioned when she was seven years old.

The latest official portrait, in 2010, was commissioned by Cunard to be displayed on the *Queen Elizabeth* liner and was painted by the youngest artist to have painted the Queen; Isobel Peachey, aged 31 at the time.

Other well-known artists who
have created official portraits of
the Queen include Rolf Harris in
2005 and Lucian Freud in 2001.

Official photographic portraits of
the Queen have been produced
by Lord Snowdon, Jane Bown
and Annie Liebovitz.

It is convention for Prince Philip
to be on the Queen's left hand
side for official photographs.

HEAD OF THE CHURCH OF ENGLAND

The Queen's titles include Defender of the Faith and the Supreme Governor of the Church of England. These signify her role as the symbolic head of the Church of England.

Princess Elizabeth was christened on 26 May 1926 and confirmed on 28 March 1942 at private chapels in Buckingham Palace and Windsor Castle respectively.

The Queen, titular Head of the Church of England, was the first British monarch to receive a visit from a pope in 450 years when Pope John Paul II visited Buckingham Palace in 1982.

There have been six popes during the Queen's reign. She has met at least three of them. They are:

Pius XII
John XXIII
Paul VI
John Paul I
John Paul II
Benedict XVI

There have also been six
Archbishops of Canterbury during
the Queen's reign. They are:

Geoffrey Fisher
Michael Ramsey
Donald Coggan
Robert Runcie
George Carey
Rowan Williams

QUEEN ELIZABETH II'S TRAVELS

Queen Elizabeth II is the most widely travelled head of state in history.

Princess Elizabeth celebrated
her twenty-first birthday with her
parents in Cape Town, during her
first state visit to South Africa.

In 1953–54 Queen Elizabeth II made
a six-month round-the-world tour
with Prince Philip, becoming the first
reigning monarch to circumnavigate
the globe, as well as the first to visit
Australia, New Zealand and Fiji.

In 1995 the Queen became
the first monarch to visit post-
apartheid South Africa.

In 1957 she made a state visit to
the United States, and in 1959
she made a tour of Canada.

In 1961 the Queen toured India
and Pakistan for the first time.

When Queen Elizabeth II and Prince
Philip visited Australia and New
Zealand in 1970, they undertook
their first 'Royal walkabout' so they
could meet a wide range of people.

To commemorate the American
Bicentennial in July 1976, the
Queen and Prince Philip visited
Philadelphia where they presented
the American people with a replica
of the Liberty Bell, known as the
Bicentennial Bell. They were given the
Freedom of the City by the Mayor.

In May 2011, the Queen became the first British monarch to visit Ireland since it had left the United Kingdom. She was also the first British monarch to meet an Irish head of state when she met Mary Robinson in 1993.

The Queen makes two overseas state visits per year and has made over 60 state visits during her reign. She has made state visits to most European countries and to many outside Europe.

The Queen has travelled overseas
more than 325 times.
She has travelled around the world
in a single tour a total of six times.

When travelling overseas, the Queen
does not use or require a passport,
as they are issued in her name.

The Queen is fluent in French and often uses this skill during state visits, such as to French-speaking Canada. She learnt the language as a child from her French and Belgian governesses.

MARRIAGE

As Queen regnant, the Queen rules in her own right and her husband, Prince Philip, does not share her rank, title, or sovereignty.

The Queen and Prince Philip first met
in 1934, but it was not until 1939 when
Elizabeth's family were touring the
Royal Naval College at Dartmouth,
and Earl Mountbatten asked Philip
to escort Elizabeth and her sister
Margaret, that they fell in love.

Both the Queen and Prince Philip
are descendants of Christian IX
of Denmark and Louise of Hesse-
Kassel and Queen Victoria and Prince
Albert. They are second cousins
once removed, and third cousins.

Elizabeth and Philip were
married on 20 November 1947 at
Westminster Abbey in London.

It is the only time in British
history that the current heir
presumptive has married.

The Queen's wedding dress was
designed by Sir Norman Hartnell
of Mayfair, London, who worked on
the same street where Her Majesty
was born. As rationing was still going
on at the time of the wedding, the
Queen had to collect ration coupons
for the fabric for her dress.

On her wedding day, the Queen wore a
tiara made for her grandmother, Queen
Mary, Queen Consort of George V.

The Queen Mary Fringe Tiara was accidentally broken on the morning of the wedding. Luckily, the court jeweller was to hand in case of emergency and, under police escort, he took the tiara to his work rooms and fixed it in time for the wedding.

They had eight bridesmaids and two kilted page boys.

The eight bridesmaids were:

Princess Margaret
Princess Alexandra
Lady Elizabeth Lambart
Lady Caroline Montagu-Douglas-Scott
Lady Mary Cambridge
The Hon. Margaret Elphinstone
The Hon. Pamela Mountbatten
The Hon. Diana Bowes-Lyon

The two page boys were:

Prince Michael of Kent
Prince William of Gloucester

The menu at the Queen's wedding to Prince Philip was Filet de Sole Mountbatten, Perdreau en Casserole and Bombe Glacée Princess Elizabeth.

When the Queen ascended to the throne, she did not take the name of Philip's royal house, but remained part of the House of Windsor.

In 2007, Queen Elizabeth II was the first British monarch to celebrate sixty years of marriage. The Queen has the longest-serving and oldest consort.

CORONATION

Elizabeth was crowned Queen
of the United Kingdom, Canada,
Australia, New Zealand, South
Africa, Ceylon and Pakistan at
Westminster Abbey on 2 June 1953.

At the coronation, Queen Elizabeth II was crowned by the Archbishop of Canterbury with St Edward's Crown. It is made of gold and decorated with a dazzling collection of precious and semi-precious stones, altogether weighing a substantial 2.23 kg.

Some of the other items of the Crown Jewels, or Regalia, which are part of the coronation ceremony include the Sovereign's Orb, which represents the monarch's role as Defender of the Faith, and two sceptres: the Sovereign's Sceptre, representing the monarch's temporal authority under the cross, and the Sceptre with Dove, representing equity, mercy, and the monarch's spiritual authority under the cross.

Her Majesty's coronation was the first to be televised. It was also filmed in 3D.

The first non-stop flight from England to Canada was made in order to transport footage of the Queen's coronation to her Canadian subjects.

The Queen's coronation brought about some major developments in televisual technology, including a new type of microphone and the Suppressed Frame system of telerecording.

Half a million extra television sets were sold in the run-up to the Queen's coronation.

More than 8,000 guests from all around the world attended the Queen's coronation at Westminster Abbey.

The Maids of Honour at Queen Elizabeth II's coronation were told to carry smelling salts inside their white gloves in case they felt faint during the ceremony.

At the lunch, a new dish was invented, named 'coronation chicken'. It was created by Constance Spry for guests from around the world. Herbs and spices were still scarce following the war so it was a very basic recipe using cold chicken pieces in a curry cream sauce with rice, peas and mixed herbs.

THE CROWN
JEWELS AND
PERSONAL
JEWELLERY
COLLECTION

The Queen owns the world's
finest pink diamond, which forms
the centre of a flower brooch.

The official Crown Jewels of the
United Kingdom are only worn at
coronations and are never taken
abroad. Some of them are used
at the Opening of Parliament.

The current display of the Crown Jewels,
or Regalia, at the Tower of London
was opened by the Queen in 1994 and
includes sceptres, orbs, rings, swords,
bracelets and St Edward's Crown.

The oldest piece of the Regalia
is the twelfth-century Anointing
Spoon made of gold, used to anoint
the sovereign with holy oil.

When she became Queen, Elizabeth
requested that a representation of
St Edward's Crown should replace
the Tudor Crown as a symbol of
the sovereign's authority. The main
difference is the raised arches
on top of St Edward's Crown,
which the Tudor Crown lacks.

The Queen has her own personal
collection of jewels from which
she often wears pieces for formal
occasions. It contains some of
the world's largest diamonds,
emeralds, sapphires and rubies.

In 1947, Queen Elizabeth II's father
gave her a wedding present of two
exquisite pearl necklaces. One is said
to have belonged to Queen Anne,
and the other to Queen Caroline,
Queen Consort to George II.

The Queen has sometimes been
seen wearing a set of three bow
brooches that consist of more
than 500 diamonds. They were
commissioned by Queen Victoria and
are now valued at over £200,000.

The Queen was given a Cartier diamond
tiara by her mother on her eighteenth
birthday. She lent this same tiara to
Catherine Middleton for her wedding
in 2011. The Cartier tiara was made in
1936 and given to the Queen Mother
by her husband, King George VI.

The Crown Jewels include the two
largest polished gems from the largest
rough gem-quality stone ever found,
the Cullinan diamond. These gems
are known as Cullinan I and II. The
next two largest gems from the stone,
Cullinan III and IV, are part of the
Queen's personal jewellery collection.

THE
COMMONWEALTH

The Queen's first Commonwealth
tour began on 24 November 1953
when she visited many countries,
travelling a total of 43,618 miles.

Within the Commonwealth of Nations, there are sixteen Commonwealth realms of which the Queen is head of state.

The Commonwealth realms are Antigua and Barbuda, Australia, The Bahamas, Barbados, Belize, Canada, Granada, Jamaica, New Zealand, Papua New Guinea, Saint Kitts and Nevis, Saint Lucia, Saint Vincent and the Grenadines, the Solomon Islands, Tuvalu, and the United Kingdom of Great Britain and Northern Ireland.

The Queen is the Head of the
Commonwealth of Nations, a
collection of 54 independent states,
nearly all of which were formerly
part of the British Empire.

She regularly attends Commonwealth
Heads of Government meetings.

In Tok Pisin, one of the official
languages of Papua New Guinea, the
Queen is known as 'Missis Kwin'.

The Queen inherited the Maori title,
Te Kotuku Rerengathi, meaning
'rare white heron of single flight',
from her father upon accession.

The Queen's Baton Relay is a relay
that starts and ends at Buckingham
Palace, travelling around the world
and then returning for the Opening
Ceremony of the Commonwealth
Games. It has been a part of the
Commonwealth Games since 1958.

When a general election was called
unexpectedly in 1974, the Queen's
tour of Australia had to be cut short for
her to return to the United Kingdom.

In 1960 the Queen had a personal flag
created, depicting a gold, crowned
letter E surrounded by gold roses on
a blue background. At first it was used
as a personal symbol, unassociated
with her role as sovereign, but it
has now come to represent her in
Commonwealth nations that are
not Commonwealth realms.

THE QUEEN
AND THE
ARMED
FORCES

The Queen is Commander-in-Chief
of the Armed Forces of the UK,
and of the Canadian Forces.

The Queen's Guard at Buckingham
Palace wear bearskin hats
which are made from the fur
of Canadian brown bears.

The Queen's Regiment was formed
as a 'large regiment' on 31 December
1966. This was an amalgamation of the
four remaining regiments of the Home
Counties Brigade, brought about as a
consequence of the Defence Review
of 1957. The four regiments formed
four battalions, retaining their previous
names in their titles. These were:

1st Battalion (Queen's Surreys)
– formerly The Queen's Royal
Surrey Regiment (2nd, 31st &
70th Regiments of Foot).

2nd Battalion (Queen's Own Buffs)
– formerly The Queen's Own Buffs,
The Royal Kent Regiment (3rd,
50th & 97th Regiments of Foot).

3rd Battalion (Royal Sussex) –
formerly the Royal Sussex Regiment
(35th & 107th Regiments of Foot).

4th Battalion (Middlesex) – formerly
the Middlesex Regiment (Duke
of Cambridge's Own) (57th &
77th Regiments of Foot).

In February 1945, during World War Two, the then Princess Elizabeth joined the Women's Auxiliary Territorial Service, where she was an auto mechanic and driver.

She qualified as a truck driver, making her first journey in a camouflaged truck from Camberley to Buckingham Palace on her own.

While in the army, Princess Elizabeth was known as No. 230873 Second Subaltern Elizabeth Windsor.

From 1964 to 2011, the Queen held the title of Lord High Admiral of the Royal Navy. In 2011 she conferred the title to her consort, Prince Philip, to celebrate his 90th birthday.

THE GOVERNMENT

The Queen is a 'constitutional monarch' which means that she is head of the state but the country is run by the government. The Queen formally approves all government legislation, advised by the Prime Minister.

The Privy Council is an advisory body to
the Queen which includes the Cabinet,
former senior politicians and judges.

The Queen meets with the Prime
Minister every week at 6.30 p.m.
on a Wednesday. If one of them is
unable to attend the meeting they
will speak on the telephone.

Over the course of the Queen's reign, twelve prime ministers of the United Kingdom have served. These are:

Sir Winston Churchill 1952–1955
Sir Anthony Eden 1955–1957
Harold Macmillan 1957–1963
Sir Alec Douglas-Home 1963–1964
Harold Wilson 1964–1970
Sir Edward Heath 1970–1974
Harold Wilson (second term) 1974–1976
James Callaghan 1976–1979
Baroness Margaret Thatcher 1979–1990
Sir John Major 1990–1997
Tony Blair 1997–2007
Gordon Brown 2007–2010
David Cameron 2010–present

Tony Blair was the first prime minister to serve who had been born whilst the Queen was on the throne. He was born on 6 May 1953, a month before the coronation.

It is believed that the Queen's favourite prime ministers were Winston Churchill, Harold Macmillan and Harold Wilson, although of course she has never expressed this opinion and all meetings are wholly confidential.

The Queen gives a speech at the annual State Opening of Parliament, outlining the legislative agenda for the year, but the speech is written by ministers. She has attended every State Opening of Parliament under her reign, except for when she was pregnant with her last two children, Andrew and Edward.

The Queen's many years of experience with prime ministers and world leaders means that she is knowledgeable on a breadth of world issues. She has developed friendships with many foreign leaders, including Nelson Mandela, George H. W. Bush and Mary Robinson.

In her memoirs, Margaret Thatcher described her weekly meetings with the Queen as '… quietly businesslike,' adding, 'Her Majesty brings to bear a formidable grasp of current issues and breadth of experience.'

In 1999, the Queen opened both
the National Assembly for Wales
and the Scottish Parliament; both
huge steps towards the devolution
of power in the United Kingdom.

All laws in the UK are upheld in the
Queen's name. Therefore, criminal
and civil proceedings cannot be taken
against Her Majesty, though she always
acts in strict accordance with the law.

SPECIAL CEREMONIES

Each year on the second Saturday in June, to celebrate the Queen's official birthday, all seven regiments of the Household Division Guards participate in the Queen's Birthday Parade known as 'Trooping the Colour'.

As Prince Philip's birthday is 10 June, on some years (as in 2006) it coincides with the Queen's official birthday.

The 'colours' flown at the Queen's Birthday Parade are one of the Regiment's flags or banners carrying all of the Regiment's battle honours, and usually one of the five regiments of Foot Guards display their 'colours'.

The only year the Queen has missed
Trooping the Colour was in 1955,
when the parade was cancelled
due to a national rail strike.

Every year at 'Trooping the Colour'
from 1969 to 1986 the Queen rode the
same black mare named Burmese.

Since the retirement of Burmese, the Queen has not ridden a horse but used Queen Victoria's 1842 ivory-clad phaeton for Trooping the Colour.

The Queen has attended over fifty Royal Maundy services at more than forty different cathedrals and abbeys across the UK. Over 6,000 elderly people have been presented with special silver coins in recognition of their work within the community.

King George V began the custom
of giving Maundy money in 1932;
it derives from the story of the Last
Supper when Jesus instructed his
disciples to love one another, and
washed their feet – a ceremony which
continues in some churches to this day.

The number of Maundy coins handed out at the annual ceremony on Maundy Thursday, the Thursday before Easter, is the same as the number of years of the Queen's life, for both men and women. So in 2011, 85 male and 85 female recipients participated, receiving the specially minted coins.

On Remembrance Sunday in November every year, the Queen lays a wreath at the Cenotaph. She has only missed six times, when she was pregnant or overseas on official visits.

In 2009, the Queen attended her first Swan Upping ceremony, the first to be attended by a monarch in centuries.

The Queen owns all unmarked mute swans in open water. During the historic Swan Upping ceremony she is saluted as 'Seigneur of the Swans' by her Swan Uppers. 'Swan Upping' dates from the twelfth century when the crown claimed all the unowned mute swans in England, ensuring a supply of meat for banquets and feasts. The Royal Family no longer eats swans and are supportive of their conservation.

Following the terrorist attacks on 11 September 2001, the Queen gave special permission for the American National Anthem to be played during the Changing of the Guard at Buckingham Palace.

SILVER AND GOLDEN JUBILEES

For her Silver Jubilee in 1977,
celebrating 25 years on the throne,
the Queen undertook six tours of
the UK, visiting 36 counties.

The Jubilee line of London
Underground was originally planned
to be called the Fleet line, but was
renamed for the Silver Jubilee.

In 2002 the Queen celebrated her
Golden Jubilee, marking 50 years
since her accession to the throne.
Over the year she made extensive
tours of the Commonwealth Realms.

Thousands gathered outside Buckingham Palace for the 'Party at the Palace'; a large concert featuring famous musicians from across the British Isles. This was followed by a national service of thanksgiving held the next day at St Paul's Cathedral.

For the Golden Jubilee, a new dish was devised and approved by the Queen, named Jubilee chicken. It was intended as a radical twist on coronation chicken and was distributed to guests at the concerts. The recipe comprises pieces of chicken marinated in lime and ginger, served cold in a white sauce of crème fraiche and mayonnaise.

The Jubilee Odyssey, a roller coaster
at Fantasy Island amusement park
in Lincolnshire, was opened by the
Queen's cousin, Prince Edward,
Duke of Kent, to commemorate
the Golden Jubilee. It is the third
tallest roller coaster in the UK.

The Empire State Building in New
York was illuminated in royal purple
and gold as a tribute to the Queen
in her Golden Jubilee year.

On 6 October 2002, while on her
Golden Jubilee tour in Canada, the
Queen dropped the ceremonial first
puck in a hockey game between the
Vancouver Canucks and the San
Jose Sharks. Over 50 years before,
in 1951, the then Princess Elizabeth
had watched her first NHL game at
Maple Leaf Gardens in Canada.

For the Golden Jubilee, several new statues of Her Majesty were unveiled. Two of these showed the Queen on horseback: one in Windsor Great Park, which was created by the sculptor Philip Jackson, and the other in Saskatchewan, Canada, which depicts the Queen riding her horse, Burmese.

Many street parties were held around the world to celebrate Her Majesty's Golden Jubilee. Most enjoyed good weather, but one particularly notable party endured temperatures of minus 20 – it was held by scientists at Rothera Research Station on Adelaide Island, off the coast of the Antarctic Peninsula.

The Queen's Gallery is a public art gallery at Buckingham Palace showing pieces from the Royal Collection. It was extended and renovated to coincide with the Golden Jubilee, and re-opened by the Queen on 21 May 2002.

FAMILY

Queen Elizabeth II had just one sibling, Princess Margaret, who was born in 1930 and died of a stroke in February 2002, aged 71.

In 1960, the Queen became the first
reigning sovereign to have a child whilst
ruling since Queen Victoria had her
last child, Princess Beatrice, in 1857.

The Queen and Prince Philip have
four children, eight grandchildren
and one great-grandchild.

The Queen has 30 godchildren.

Queen Elizabeth II and Prince
Philip's first child, Prince Charles,
was born six days before their
first wedding anniversary.

Charles was created Prince of Wales and Earl of Chester on 26 July 1958 by his mother, the Queen, though the ceremony of his investiture as Prince would not occur until 1 July 1969.

Though the Royal House is named Windsor, it was decreed via a 1960 Order in Council that the descendants of Queen Elizabeth II and Prince Philip should have the personal surname Mountbatten-Windsor.

RESIDENCES
AND STAFF

The Queen's official residence is
Buckingham Palace in London. Other
royal residences include Windsor
Castle, the Palace of Holyroodhouse,
St James's Palace, Kensington
Palace and Clarence House.

The Queen owns Balmoral Castle
in Aberdeenshire, Scotland, and
Sandringham House in Norfolk.

The Queen enjoys time spent at
Balmoral from August to October. The
surrounding estate contains a forest,
a wildlife reserve, open countryside
and highland paths and fells. The
Queen is a fan of Scottish country
dancing, and holds dances during
her stays at Balmoral Castle.

The Queen enjoys spending Christmas with her family at their Sandringham Estate in Norfolk. The whole family goes to church on Christmas Day, and on the traditional Boxing Day pheasant shoot.

After the coronation, Elizabeth and Philip moved to Buckingham Palace. Like many of her predecessors, however, it is believed that she dislikes the Palace as a residence and considers Windsor Castle, west of London, to be her home.

When the Queen is in residence at Buckingham Palace, four foot guards stand at the front of the building. When she is away there are two.

Angela Kelly, daughter of a Liverpool dockworker and herself a Member of the Royal Victorian Order, is the Queen's Personal Assistant and Senior Dresser.

The Queen has simple taste in food
and is said to enjoy such things as
grapes, smoked haddock, cheese
with celery and barley water.

Queen Elizabeth II's favourite
drink, like the Queen Mother's, is
said to be a gin and Dubonnet.

When in residence in London, the
Queen enjoys high tea at 5 p.m.
consisting of delicate sandwiches,
Dundee cake and tea.

The Woman of the Bedchamber attends
the Queen on all public occasions. Her
role also involves replying to children's
letters, 'personal' shopping for Her
Majesty and inquiring after ill servants.

The Queen continues the custom
of her father and grandfather of
giving Christmas puddings to
staff. She has given out more
than 90,000 puddings to date.

The bagpipes are played beneath
the Queen's window at Buckingham
Palace every weekday at 9.00 a.m. for
fifteen minutes. They are also played
when the Queen is in residence at the
Palace of Holyroodhouse, Windsor
Palace and Balmoral Castle.

Every monarch since Queen Victoria
has had a Piper to the Sovereign. Since
1965, the post of Piper to the Sovereign
has been held by a serving soldier.

AWARDS, HONOURS, ROYAL WARRANTS AND PATRONAGE

On the Queen's official birthday, she announces the Birthday Honours List of those receiving honours such as CBEs, OBEs and honorific knighthoods.

The Queen has conferred over
400,000 awards and honours
since her reign began.

The Queen has held over 600
ceremonies in which people are
presented their awards and honours.
These are known as Investitures.

Royal warrants are awarded by the Queen, Prince Philip and Prince Charles, to companies or tradespeople who have provided a service or goods of excellent quality to the Royal Family for over five years.

Current royal warrant holders include
A. and F. Pears Ltd for their soap, Aston
Martin for their cars, Asprey for their
jewellery, Bendicks for their chocolates,
Britvic for their soft drinks, Carr's for
their crackers, Heinz, Kent and Sons for
hairbrushes, Kellogg's, Lyle's Golden
Syrup, Petersfield Book Shop for their
picture framing, Smythson for their
leather goods and stationery, Staples for
their beds, Suttons Seeds, and Taylors
of Harrogate for their tea and coffee.

The fashion designer Hardy Amies
designed clothes for the Queen for forty
years, including the outfits he made her
for her royal tour of Canada as princess
in 1950 and the dress she wore for
her Silver Jubilee portrait, before he
gave up the royal warrant in 1990.

In March 2004 the Queen hosted the
first women-only event, 'Women of
Achievement', at Buckingham Palace.

The Queen is the patron of
approximately 600 organisations.

LETTERS AND AUDIENCES

Since her reign began, the Queen
has received more than 3 million
items of correspondence.

In March 1976 the Queen sent her first email from the Royal Signals and Radar Establishment army base in Malvern, Worcestershire.

The Queen sends congratulatory messages to those reaching their 100th birthdays. They will receive another message at 105 and every year after that. During her reign the Queen has sent around 110,000 telegrams and messages to those celebrating their centenary.

Similarly, married couples reaching
their 60th wedding anniversary can
apply for a message from the Queen.
They can also receive a message
on their 65th and 70th anniversary,
and all anniversaries after that.
The Queen has sent over 520,000
telegrams to those celebrating
milestone wedding anniversaries.

In 2009, at the age of 109, Catherine Masters of Oxfordshire wrote a letter to the Queen complaining that the picture of the Queen in her congratulatory cards had not changed for some years – she was always wearing the same yellow dress. In a surprise response, Prince William visited Mrs Masters and apologised, and next year the picture was different.

During her reign, the Queen and Prince Philip have sent over 37,000 Christmas cards.

The Queen has a Private Secretary
to assist with her vast amount of
official correspondence. The Rt.
Hon. Sir Christopher Geidt has
held this post since 2007.

The traditional form of greeting Her
Majesty is a bow of the head from
the neck for a man, and a small
curtsy for a woman, although it is also
acceptable to shake hands instead.

If being presented to the Queen,
the correct formal address is 'Your
Majesty', followed by 'Ma'am'.

In 1956, the Queen introduced informal
luncheons at Buckingham Palace,
inviting six to eight guests from all walks
of life, which continue to this day.

The Queen and Prince Philip attend garden parties at both Buckingham Palace and Holyroodhouse. These parties typically involve around 400 waiting staff, and an average of 27,000 cups of tea are consumed.

The Queen has met several famous astronauts at Buckingham Palace, including: the first astronaut to go into space, Major Yuri Gagarin; the first woman in space, Valentina Tereshkova; the first man on the moon, Neil Armstrong; and the other Apollo 11 astronauts, Michael Collins and Edwin Aldrin.

POPULAR CULTURE

The then Princess Elizabeth made her first public broadcast as a child of fourteen on the BBC's *Children's Hour* programme in October 1940.

The Queen has made her Christmas broadcast to the Commonwealth nearly every single year of her reign. The single year she has not done so was 1969, when she issued a written message instead, due to her belief that with the investiture of Charles as Prince of Wales and the documentary, *Royal Family,* being shown, her family had been on TV enough that year.

In 2004, the Queen had a separate Christmas Message for the British Armed Forces, broadcast on the British Forces Broadcasting Service.

The Queen has attended 35 *Royal Variety Performances* in her life.

The Queen has visited the sets of
Britain's most popular soap operas,
Coronation Street (1982), *EastEnders*
(2001) and *Emmerdale* (2002).

She enjoys watching *Doctor
Who*, *Coronation Street* and
Agatha Christie's Poirot.

At the time of her coronation, the Queen's favourite actors were said to be Laurence Olivier, Gary Cooper and Dirk Bogarde.

Queen Elizabeth II was the first member of the Royal Family to receive a gold disc from the recording industry for sales of the Golden Jubilee *Party at the Palace* CD.

The first football match the Queen
attended was the 1953 FA Cup
final at Wembley Stadium, a
month before her coronation.

The Queen and Prince Philip were
present at the 1966 World Cup final,
and Her Majesty presented the trophy
to England captain Bobby Moore.

In 2004, the Queen invited the cast
of *Les Misérables* from the West
End to perform for French president
Jacques Chirac at Windsor Castle.

ANIMALS

The Queen's first corgi was called
Susan, and was a present for
her 18th birthday in 1944.

The Queen is an expert dog handler.
She uses hand signals and whistles
to control the twenty Labradors and
spaniels kept as working dogs in the
royal kennels at Sandringham.

The Queen introduced a new breed of
dog called the 'dorgi'. This is a cross
between a corgi and a dachshund.

The Queen currently has four corgis named Linnet, Monty, Willow and Holly and four dorgis named Cider, Berry, Candy and Vulcan.

The Queen is patron of a number of racing societies, including the Royal Pigeon Racing Association. She enjoys racing pigeons; an interest first sparked in the Royal Family by the gift of racing pigeons received from King Leopold II of Belgium in 1886.

The Queen is an owner and breeder
of thoroughbred racehorses.
Her horses have won at Royal
Ascot on several occasions.

The Queen's love of horses began
when she was four years old, when
she received a Shetland pony from
her grandfather, King George V.

The Queen's racing colours are a purple
body braided with gold, scarlet sleeves
and a black velvet cap with a gold fringe.

HOBBIES AND HABITS

The Queen owns one of the
world's largest private collections
of postage stamps.

The Queen enjoys detective fiction; P. D. James and Dick Francis are favourites.

The Queen is keen on photography and enjoys taking pictures of her family.

The Queen listens to Radio 4
while eating her breakfast.

The Queen is fond of jigsaw puzzles,
and was given a custom-made puzzle
by a jigsaw maker from London in
1993. The box is blank because Her
Majesty believes a picture of the
finished puzzle makes it too easy.

TRANSPORT

The Crown Equerry is in charge of
the Queen's transport which includes
thirty horses, three Rolls Royces,
Prince Philip's electrically powered
van, and various state coaches.

The most recent state car to be acquired is a Bentley, custom-made with input from the Queen, Prince Philip and their Head Chauffeur. It is nearly a metre longer and over a metre wider than normal Bentleys, and includes removable rear window covers to increase or decrease visibility for the Queen and for spectators as desired.

The Royal Train consists of one of two engines, named 'Royal Sovereign' and 'Queen's Messenger', pulling a selection of the eight custom-built saloon carriages, including The Queen's Saloon and The Duke of Edinburgh's Saloon.

When possible, the Queen does not use the Royal Train but takes normal, scheduled train services.

The Royal Household operates a
Sikorsky S-76 C++ helicopter, based at
Blackbushe Aerodrome in Hampshire.

The Gold State Coach which was
used at the Queen's coronation has
been used for every coronation since
George IV's in 1821. The coach was
actually built for George III for his
coronation but was not ready in time.

Queen Elizabeth II travelled in the
Gold State Coach for her wedding
in 1947, but it is only used for very
special occasions, the last being
the Golden Jubilee in 2002. It is
richly decorated inside and out, and
pulled by a team of eight horses.

The Queen first set sail on the
Royal Yacht *Britannia* on 1 May
1954 at Tobruk, Libya on the final
stage of her Commonwealth Tour
back to London. This yacht was
decommissioned in 1997.

THINGS NAMED FOR THE QUEEN

Princess Elizabeth Land, a sector
in Australian Antarctic Territory, was
discovered in 1931 and named by Sir
Douglas Mawson for the young princess.

Queen Elizabeth Country Park on the
South Downs in southern England
contains 2,000 acres of woodland
and downland and was formally
opened by the Queen in 1976.

Twinned with the Queen Elizabeth
Country Park, Queen Elizabeth
National Park in Uganda is nearly
2,000 square kilometres in size,
and is also named for the Queen.

The Olympic Park in London, built for the 2012 Olympics, will become known as the Queen Elizabeth Olympic Park after the games have finished, commemorating the Queen's Diamond Jubilee.

The Queen's Gardens in Croydon, London, were opened by the Queen in 1983, on the previous site of Croydon Central railway station.

The City of Elizabeth, South Australia, was, in 1963, visited by the Queen for whom it had been named back in 1955. It became part of the City of Playford in 1997.

The Queen Elizabeth Islands off the north of Canada were renamed with the coronation in 1953. They include the northernmost permanently inhabited place in the world, Alert, on Ellesmere Island, Nunavut, which hosts a weather station and a signals intelligence base.

On 9 October 2002, Dalton Digby
Wildlands Provincial Park in Canada
received a visit from the Queen
to commemorate her Golden
Jubilee, on which occasion the park
was renamed Queen Elizabeth
II Wildlands Provincial Park.

Queenstown in Singapore was
named in 1952 to commemorate
the coronation of the Queen.

Port Elizabeth on the island
of Bequia in the Grenadines
was named for the Queen.

HONORARY AND LESSER-KNOWN TITLES

The Queen is an Admiral in
the Great Navy of the State of
Nebraska, an honorary title given
in the landlocked U.S. state.

Before her accession, Her Majesty became an honorary Bachelor of Music, Doctor of Civil Law and Doctor of Music, and a Doctor of Law from both the University of London and the University of Edinburgh.

From 1947 until her accession, the Queen was a Fellow of the Royal Society. Once monarch she became the Society's patron.

Since 1947 the Queen has been a
Freeman of the Worshipful Company
of Drapers and an Honorary Member
of the Institution of Civil Engineers.

Since 1951, Her Majesty has
been an Honorary Fellow of both
the Royal College of Surgeons of
England and the Royal College of
Obstetricians and Gynaecologists.

As the reigning monarch of the Bailiwicks of Jersey and Guernsey, the Queen holds the title Duke of Normandy. The title comes from the fact that the Bailiwicks used to be part of the Duchy of Normandy. Regardless of the gender of the sovereign, they are known as the Duke.

On the Isle of Man Elizabeth II is
known as the Queen, Lord of Mann.
With the Isle of Man Purchase Act
1765 the title was revested into the
British Crown, meaning the reigning
monarch will always be Lord of Mann.

GIFTS

During her reign the Queen has received a variety of strange and interesting official gifts from other rulers and heads of state. These include:

- jaguars and sloths from Brazil
- two black beavers from Canada
- pineapples
- a canary from Germany
- a pair of cowboy boots from the USA
- a box of snail shells
- two young giant turtles from the Seychelles

- an elephant called Jumbo from Cameroon
- prawns
- a Maori canoe from New Zealand
- two floor mats from Queen Sālote and the people of Tonga
- a portrait of Her Majesty in the robes of the Most Noble Order of the Garter from Russia

THE DIAMOND JUBILEE

An extra bank holiday will occur
in the United Kingdom on 5 June
for the Diamond Jubilee to mark
60 years of the Queen's reign.

A pageant along the River Thames
will celebrate the Diamond Jubilee,
consisting of over 1,000 boats.
It will be the biggest flotilla seen
on the Thames in 350 years.

In celebration of the Diamond Jubilee,
the London borough of Greenwich was
granted status as a Royal Borough.

The official emblem for the Diamond Jubilee was created by ten-year-old Katherine Dewar from Chester.

The Woodland Trust, a charity concerned with protecting native woodland, will plant one new woodland for each year of the Queen's reign, to honour her Diamond Jubilee. One of these will be a 500-acre wood, with the other 59 being 60-acre woodlands.

KEEP THE FLAG FLYING

£4.99

ISBN: 978 1 84953 268 6

'I am very proud to be British. I'm very conscious of carrying my country with me wherever I go.'

Julie Andrews

ROUSING WORDS FOR PLUCKY PATRIOTS

When it comes to keeping a stiff upper lip, we Brits are in a league of our own. The weather may be awful and the economy might be in a state, but give us a nice cup of tea and a bit of pomp and ceremony to watch and we'll instantly remember why Britain is great.

Here's a book packed with spirited quotations to inspire upstanding citizens everywhere.

www.summersdale.com

@Summersdale